PYTHON CRASH COURSE

A PRACTICAL BEGINNER'S GUIDE TO LEARN PYTHON IN 7 DAYS OR LESS, INTRODUCING YOU INTO THE WORLD OF DATA SCIENCE, ARTIFICIAL INTELLIGENCE AND MACHINE LEARNING, WITH HANDS-ON PROJECTS

ERICK THOMPSON

TABLE OF CONTENTS

INTRODUCTION

Python is a significant level programming language, normally utilized for general purposes. It was initially developed by Guido van Rossum at the "Middle Wiskunde and Informatica (CWI), Netherlands," during the 1980s and presented by the "Python Software Foundation" in 1991. It was planned essentially to underscore comprehensibility of programming code, and its linguistic structure empowers developers to pass on thoughts utilizing less lines of code. Python programming language speeds up activity while taking into account higher productivity in making framework reconciliations. Designers are utilizing Python for "web advancement (server-side), programming improvement, arithmetic, framework scripting."

With the presentation of different upgrades, for example, "list appreciation" and a "trash assortment framework," which can gather reference cycles, the Python 2.0 was propelled in the last quarter of 2000. Thusly, in 2008, Python 3.0 was discharged as a significant rendition overhaul within reverse similarity taking into consideration the Python 2.0 code to be executed on Python 3.0 without requiring any adjustments. Python is bolstered by a network of software engineers that ceaselessly create and keep up the "CPython," which is an open-source reference usage. The "Python Software Foundation" is a not revenue driven association that is liable for overseeing and coordinating assets for creating Python programming just as "CPython."

Here is a portion of the key highlights of Python that render it as the language of decision for coding beginners as well as advanced programming software engineers alike:

1. Readability: Python peruses a great deal like the English language, which adds to its simplicity of coherence.

2. Learnability: Python is a significant level programming language and considered simple to learn because of the capacity to code utilizing the English language like articulations, which infers it is easy to appreciate and, in this way, become familiar with the language.

3. Operating Systems: Python is effectively open and can be worked across various Operating frameworks including Linux, Unix, Mac, Windows among others. This renders Python as an adaptable and cross-stage language.

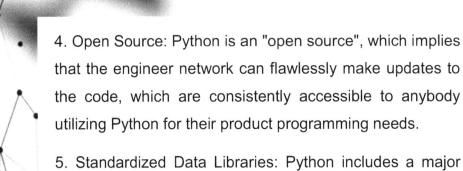

4. Open Source: Python is an "open source", which implies that the engineer network can flawlessly make updates to the code, which are consistently accessible to anybody utilizing Python for their product programming needs.

5. Standardized Data Libraries: Python includes a major standard information library with an assortment of helpful codes and functionalities that can be utilized when composing Python code for information examination and advancement of AI models.

6. Free: Considering the wide appropriateness and use of Python, it is difficult to accept that it keeps on being openly accessible for simple download and use. This suggests anybody hoping to learn or utilize Python can just download and utilize it for their applications totally complimentary. Python is in reality an ideal case of a "FLOSS (Free/Libre Open Source Software)", which implies one could "uninhibitedly convey duplicates of this product, read its source code and alter it."

7. Supports overseeing special cases: An "exemption" can be characterized as "an occasion that can happen during program exemption and can disturb the typical progression of the program." Python is fit for supporting the treatment of these "exemptions," inferring that you could compose less blunder inclined codes and test your code with an

assortment of cases, which might prompt a "special case" later on.

8. Advanced Features: Python can likewise bolster "generators and rundown appreciations."

9. Storage administration: Python is likewise ready to help "programmed memory the executives," which infers that the capacity memory will be cleared and made accessible consequently. You are not required to clear and let lose the framework memory.

Applications:

1. Web planning – Some of the generally utilized web structures, for example, "Django" and "Flagon" have been created utilizing Python. These structures help the designer recorded as a hard copy server-side codes that empower the board of database, age of backend programming rationale, planning of URL, among others. AI – An assortment of AI models has been composed solely in Python. AI is a path for machines to compose rationale so as to learn and fix a particular issue all alone. For example, Python-based AI calculations utilized being developed of "item proposal frameworks" for eCommerce organizations, for example, Amazon, Netflix, YouTube and some more. Different cases of Python-based AI models are the facial acknowledgment and the voice

acknowledgment innovations accessible on our cell phones.

2. Data Analysis – Python can likewise be utilized in the advancement of information perception and information investigation instruments and procedures, for example, disperse plots and other graphical portrayals of information.

3. "Scripting" – It can be characterized as the way toward producing basic projects for mechanization of direct undertakings like those required to send robotized email reactions and instant messages. You could build up these sorts of programming utilizing the Python programming language.

4. Gaming Industry – A wide assortment of gaming programs have been created with the utilization of Python.

5. Python additionally bolsters the advancement of "implanted applications."

6. Desktop applications – You could utilize information libraries, for example, "Tinder" or "QT" to make work area applications dependent on Python.

CHAPTER - 1
THE WORLD OF DATA SCIENCE
TECHNOLOGIES

Data science

If you work with data, then Data Visualization is an important part of your daily routine. And if you happen to use Python programming language for your analysis, you must be overwhelmed by the sheer number of choices available in the form of data visualization libraries

How to Generate Data

Data visualization includes numerous equipment for generating information. The equipment used in the technology of visualized records in Python include the following:

Cluvio

Ever needed for a device that may permit the introduction of thrilling visualizations? Cluvio might be the device which you have been looking for. Cluvio is a corporation based totally in Germany that was founded in 2016. It offers thrilling and excellent features for its users and allows you to execute SQL queries from your database.

More than 100 groups accept as true with this tool of records visualization due to various reasons:

Amazing usability and design. Cluvio has an exquisite design for its customers this is of good excellent and an easy interface for the novice Python programmers to apprehend. The design has high requirements that allow the advent of interactive models. Supports the analysis of SQL-primarily based records. It analyzes any structured question language statistics, generates charts, and shares them out which is not seen on other gear for generating records. Creates interactive forums. Interactive dashboards are more often than not preferred by means of users. Cluvio generates interactive boards that make facts visualization thrilling for Python beginners. Supports each R language and SQL. Cluvio integrates with each SQL and R languages which makes it a powerful device. It is able to generate green statistical data using the R language that maximum records engineers use in records visualization.

This makes the tool greater famous than different tools.

Suitable for each small and huge organizations. Cluvio consists of various pricing alternatives that desire both the infant organizations and the major agencies. It has an unfastened pricing option plan, a starter plan, and also a seasoned plan for the big corporations. Each of the plans has different features for its users.

One of the downsides of Cluvio is that it does no longer help different file codecs which include the CSV and the Excel formats.

Google charts

You have all heard of Google, proper? Google offers sizable tools for its users across the world that help within the running and execution of facts. A Google chart is one of the equipment being presented that assists you in your management and in the presentation of information. Google charts constitute and generate your statistics inside the shape of pie charts and pictographs. This makes it simpler for customers to examine the records and make the evaluation. Google charts are unfastened gear that makes them popular compared to other equipment which can be provided at a rate.

Moreover, Google charts do no longer require any programming abilities so as to use them. It normally favors the amateur Python programmers who do no longer have adequate programming skills in view that they're just starting up their programming journey. They are capable of generating visualized information from statistical graphs and pie charts.

Google charts also offer the benefit of free virtualization hosting for its users at no cost. This enables the sharing of data across the website. Google charts also allow programmers to generate on their photographs from charts and different plots by the use of an API (Application Programming Interface) referred to as the Image Charts API. With this API, you're best required to set up a URL on the way to include your statistics on the facts and its formatting. You do no longer require any type of coding to be able to generate a photo from a Google chart.

Its main downside is that it has a poor guide for its clients, in contrast to other gear of data visualization. Also, there might also be possibilities of the loss of your images in situations in which the Google servers are down. Many of the beginner Python programmers suffer this on the grounds that they neglect to again up their images. The final drawback of a Google chart is that it denies its customers the capability to carry out a few modifications on their code since the code isn't quite exposed.

Infogram

This is a device used to generate information from advertising. It has excessive competencies for publishing compared to the equipment cited above. In fogram is much famous for its simplicity to apply because it contains a person-friendly interface for the newbie Python programmers to apprehend. It additionally offers terrific help for customers in contrast to its far visible on other gear together with the Google charts. In fogram is normally preferred with the aid of the managers and the software engineers involved in the information virtualization.

Infogrames focus on pix as a way to generate statistics. They offer its customers with templates that permit customization based on the statistical information and any sort of pix. It is obtainable at a rate of approximately $19 per person every month. This makes it incorrect for not the well-established firms. Its performance isn't quite functional compared to a different gear.

Visme

This is a device used for the design of shared stories in a manner of shows. Visme consists of three pricing plans which encompass the individual plan, the enterprise plan, and the education plan. Most people utilize this device due to its simple user interface that provides ease of use. Visme also provides extensive graphs and resources that assist within the advent of stable and attractive models. It additionally offers good high-quality customer support that allows in supporting the novice Python programmers.

The downside concerned for this tool include troubles with the text boxes and varying fine of the layout while files are exported. This makes it tough for beginners to use. Individuals who mostly opt for this tool are the advertising directors and also the persons involved in media productions.

Flare

This is an ActionScript library that allows customers to create any form of virtualization from the charts to something interactive. Flare permits you to make displays of the charts in an affordable manner. Users additionally have the capability of creating customizations at the dashboards via using text bins on the way to point out the insights.

The downside of this tool is that the virtualization made while using this device is quite flawed for cellular packages. It is additionally hard to integrate this device with a few website programs. Mores, the flare device takes time to be up to date and it, therefore, produces outdated dashboards not forgetting the many bugs it contains.

How to Download Data?

Gone are the times when maximum of the amateur Python programmers experienced tough times while downloading their visualized records. It has been thankfully made less complicated nowadays to attract your records with the aid of imposing some modules. The modules being talked about right here are Pandas and Matplotlib.

Let us now get into details at the numerous modules to help you download your Python records.

Pandas

They are Python packages with several tools for analyzing records.

Pandas are used for the management and importation of datasets in Python using lots of codecs. They also are included with some of the strategies which can assist within the fact's analysis in Python.

Many individuals choose the use of pandas in facts visualization because of the following reasons:

They allow facts presentation in a manner that may be without problems analyzed. They do this via the usage of the Series statistics structure and also Data Frame records structure.

Pandas encompass a number of techniques suitable for the efficient filtering of data.

They additionally contain a fixed of utilities that guide the enter and output operations. Pandas can study the distinctive formats of facts such as CSV and additionally MS excel.

How can you put it in pandas?

Pandas do now not include the regular Python distributions. You need to put in them to your terminal to use them. This can be accomplished by the usage of the pip command that typically comes with the Python distribution. Run the pip command together with pandas on the terminal of your system.

In conditions where you have got anaconda already set up on your gadget, you could run the conda command collectively with the pandas for your terminal to make the set up successful. You are advised to put in the trendy version of pandas for your gadget. You are now equipped to go.

Let us now dig deeper into the styles of data systems noted above that are used by pandas in Python.

Series

This form of information structure is similar to a one-dimensional array. A series of information systems gives garage to any sort of information, and its values can't be changed. The first detail of the information shape is normally assigned an index fee of 0 while the ultimate element is assigned an index of N-1. N represents the total amount of factors within the information structure.

To first establish the Pandas collection:

You want to import the pandas' bundle to your terminal.

Series is then created with the aid of the usage of an array after calling on the pd. Series () technique.

The contents of the Series will finally be displayed after walking at the print () command.

The output of the content material will include columns, whereby the primary column can be the indexes of the elements, while the second column will contain the elements used in the array.

A collection also can be generated by using the use of the numpy array then, later on, made some conversion to a Pandas series. This is how it may be accomplished.

#import on pandas on your terminal.

#import on numpy.

#import on the system command.

#call on the file object for the output to be displayed by the print () method.

#call on the numpy library to create an array of your elements #assign an array to the Pandas series.

#call on the print method to display the output.

The output will contain a primary column with the indexes of the factors, and the second column can be elements of your array.

Data Frame

This form of facts shape in pandas is in the shape of a desk that displays information within the phrases of rows and columns. It is a 2-dimensional array, in contrast to what is visible inside the Series records shape. The values of the columns may be changed without affecting their identities.

Data Frame records systems can be generated from scratch, or you may determine to use on the numpy library and convert them later to the facts structure.

By constructing from scratch, you could follow the subsequent steps:

#import pandas in your terminal #create a Data Frame.

#assign Data Frame to a variable the use of pandas wherein you furthermore may assign the values of the rows and columns as part of your arguments. #name at the print method to show the output.

CHAPTER - 2
CUSTOMER TARGETING AND
SEGMENTATION

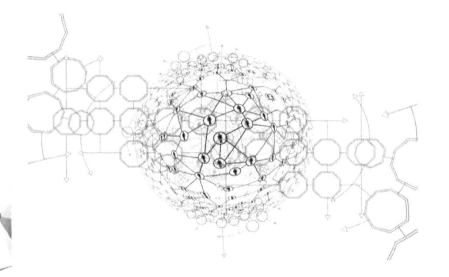

For the advertising organizations to have the option to arrive at their clients with an elevated level of personalization, they are required to target progressively granular sections. The man-made brainpower innovation can draw on the current client information and train Machine learning calculations against "highest quality level" preparing sets to recognize normal properties and critical factors. The information sections could be as basic as area, sexual orientation, and age, or as perplexing as the purchaser's persona and past conduct. With AI, Dynamics Segmentation is attainable which represents the way that clients' practices are ever-changing, and individuals can take on various personas in various circumstances.

Deals and Marketing Forecast

One of the clearest computerized reasoning applications in promoting is in the advancement of deals and advertising gauging models. The high volume of quantifiable information, for example, clicks, buys, email reactions, and time spent on website pages fill in as preparing assets for the AI calculations. A portion of the main business knowledge and creation organizations in the market are Sisense, RapidMiner, and Birst. Advertising organizations are constantly overhauling their promoting endeavors, and with the assistance of AI and AI, they can anticipate the accomplishment of their showcasing activities or email crusades. Man-made consciousness innovation can examine past deals information, monetary patterns just as industrywide correlations with foresee short and long-haul deals execution and estimate deals results. The business conjectures model guide in the estimation of item request and to assist organizations with dealing with their creation to upgrade deals.

Automatic Advertisement Targeting

With the presentation of computerized reasoning innovation, offering on and focusing on program-based commercial has gotten essentially increasingly effective. Automatic publicizing can be characterized as "the mechanized procedure of purchasing and selling promotion stock to a trade which interfaces sponsors to distributers." To permit constant offering for stock across web-based social networking stations and cell phones just as TV, man-made reasoning innovation is utilized. This likewise returns to prescient examination and the capacity to display information that could beforehand just be resolved retroactively. Man-made consciousness can help the best time to serve a specific promotion, the likelihood of an advertisement transforming into deals, the responsiveness of the client, and the probability of commitment with the advertisement.

Automatic organizations can assemble and investigate visiting clients' information and practices to streamline ongoing efforts and to focus on the crowd all the more correctly. Automatic media purchasing incorporates the utilization of "interest side stages" (to encourage the way toward purchasing advertisement stock on the open market) and "information the executives' stages" (to give the promoting organization a capacity to arrive at their intended interest group). So as to enable the promoting rep to settle on educated choices with respect to their planned clients, the information the executive's stages are intended to gather and break down the enormous volume of site "treat information." For instance, web crawler showcasing (SEM) publicizing rehearsed by channels like Facebook, Twitter, and Google. To productively oversee tremendous stock of the site and application watchers, automatic promotions give a critical edge over contenders. Google and Facebook fill in as the best quality level for productive and powerful publicizing and are equipped to words giving an easy to understand stage that will permit non-specialized advertising organizations to begin, run and measure their drives and crusades on the web.

Visual Search and Image Recognition

A long way of the progressions in man-made brainpower-based picture acknowledgment and examination innovation has brought about uncanny visual pursuit functionalities. With the presentation of innovation like Google Lens and stages like Pinterest, individuals would now be able to discover results that are outwardly like each other utilizing the visual hunt usefulness. The visual inquiry works similarly as customary content put together quests that show results with respect to a comparable theme. Significant retailers and promoting organizations are progressively utilizing the visual pursuit to offer an improved and all the more captivating client experience. Visual pursuit can be utilized to improve promoting and give item suggestions dependent on the style of the item rather than the buyer's previous conduct or buys.

Significant ventures have been made by Target and Asks in the visual quest innovation advancement for their web-based business site. In 2017, Target reported an organization with intrigue that permits incorporation of Pinterest's visual pursuit application called "Pinterest focal point" into Target's portable application. Accordingly, customers can snap a photo of items that they might want to buy while they are all over town and find comparable things on Target's online business website. Essentially, the visual pursuit application propelled by Asks called "Asks' Style Match" permits customers to snap a photograph or transfer a picture on the Asks site or application and quest their item index for comparative things. These apparatuses draw in customers to retailers for things that they may run over in a magazine or while making the rounds by helping them to look for the perfect item regardless of whether they don't have the foggiest idea what the item is.

Picture acknowledgment has hugely helped showcasing organizations to increase an edge via web-based networking media by permitting them to discover an assortment of employments of their image logos and items in staying aware of the visual patterns. This wonder is additionally called "visual social tuning in" and permits organizations to distinguish and get where and how clients are collaborating with their image, logo, and item in any event, when the organization isn't alluded straightforwardly by its name.

Marketing and Advertising

An AI calculation created because of enormous information investigation can be effortlessly prepared with writings, stills, and video portions as information sources. It would then be able to extricate articles and ideas from these sources and suggest effective showcasing and publicizing arrangements. For instance, an apparatus called "Laban" was created by Alibaba that can make pennants at lightning speed in contrast with a human originator. In 2016, for the Chinese web-based shopping spectacle called "Singles Day," Laban produced a hundred and 17 million standard structures at a speed of 8000 pennant plans for every second.

The "twentieth Century Fox" teamed up with IBM to utilize their AI framework "Watson" for the making of the trailer of their blood and gore film "Morgan." To gain proficiency with the fitting "minutes" or clasps that ought to show up in a standard thriller trailer, Watson was prepared to group and examine input "minutes" from various media and other piece components from over a hundred thrillers. This preparation brought about the production of a six-minute film trailer by Watson in a minor 24 hours, which would have taken human expert weeks to create.

With the utilization of Machine learning, PC vision innovation, common language preparing, and prescient examination, the promoting procedure can be quickened exponentially through an AI showcasing stage. For instance, the man-made consciousness based promoting stage created by Albert Intelligence Marketing can produce self-ruling effort the board procedures, make custom arrangements and perform crowd focusing on. The organization revealed a 183% improvement in client exchange rate and over 600% higher discussion effectiveness credited to the utilization of their AI-based stage.

In March 2016, the computerized reasoning based innovative executive called "man-made intelligence CD ß" was propelled by McCann Erickson Japan as the primary mechanical inventive chief at any point created. "Man-made intelligence CD ß" was given preparing on select components of different TV shows and the victors from the previous 10 years of All Japan Radio and Television CM celebration. With the utilization of information mining capacities, "simulated intelligence CD ß" can extricate thoughts and subjects satisfying each customer's individual crusade needs.

CHAPTER - 3
APPLICATION OF MACHINE LEARNING
UTILIZING SCIKIT-LEARN LIBRARY

To see how Scikit-Learn library is utilized in the improvement of machine calculation, let us utilize the "Sales_Win_Loss informational index from IBM's Watson vault" containing information acquired from deals battle of a discount provider of car parts. We will fabricate a Machine model to anticipate which deals crusade will be a champ and which will bring about misfortune.

The informational index can be imported utilizing Pandas and investigated utilizing Pandas methods, for example, "head (), tail (), and types ()." The plotting procedures from "Seaborn" will be utilized to imagine the information. To process the information Scikit-Lean's "preprocessing. Label Encoder ()" will be utilized and "train_test_split ()" to separate the informational collection into preparing subset and testing subset.

To create expectations from our informational index, three unique calculations will be utilized, to be specific, "Straight Support Vector Classification and K-closest neighbors' classifier." To think about the exhibitions of these calculations Scikit-Learn library procedure "accuracy score" will be utilized. The presentation score of the models can be imagined utilizing Scikit-Learn and "Yellow brick" perception.

Importing the Data Set

To import the "Sales_Win_Loss informational index from IBM's Watson archive," initial step is bringing in the "Pandas" module utilizing "import pandas as pd."

At that point we influence a variable URL as "https://community.watsonanalytics.com/wp content/transfers/2015/04/WA_Fn-UseC_-Sales-Win-Loss.csv" to store the URL from which the informational index will be downloaded.

Presently, "reads () as sales data = predocs (URL)" procedure will be utilized to peruse the above "csv or comma-isolated qualities" record, which is provided by the Pandas module. The csv record will at that point be changed over into a Pandas information structure, with the outcome in factor as "sales data," where the system will be put away.

For new 'Pandas' clients, the "pd.read csv()" method in the code referenced above will produce a plain information structure called "information system", where a record for each line is contained in the main section, and the name/name for every segment in the principal line are the underlying segment names obtained from the informational collection. In the above code scrap, the "business information" variable outcomes in a table delineated in the image beneath.

In the chart over, the "row0, row1, row2" speaks to singular record list, and the "col0, col1, col2" speak to the names for singular segments or highlights of the informational index.

With this progression, you have effectively put away a duplicate of the informational collection and changed it into a "Pandas" system!

Presently, utilizing the "head () as Sales_data. head ()" procedure, the records from the information structure can be shown as appeared beneath to get a "vibe" of the data contained in the informational index.

Data Exploration

Since we have our own duplicate of the informational index, which has been changed into a "Pandas" information outline, we can rapidly investigate the information to comprehend what data can tell can be assembled from it and appropriately to design a strategy.

In any ML venture, information investigation will in general be an exceptionally basic stage. Indeed, even a quick informational collection investigation can offer us critical data that could be barely noticeable something else, and this data can propose noteworthy inquiries that we would then be able to endeavor to answer utilizing our venture.

Some outsider Python libraries will be utilized here to help us with the handling of the information so we can effectively utilize this information with the amazing calculations of Scikit-Learn. Indeed, "(head)" is viably fit for doing substantially more than showing information records and redo the "head ()" procedure to show just a chose records with orders like "sales data. head(n=2)". This order will specifically show the initial 2 records of the informational collection. At a snappy look clearly

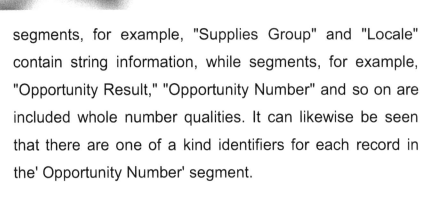

segments, for example, "Supplies Group" and "Locale" contain string information, while segments, for example, "Opportunity Result," "Opportunity Number" and so on are included whole number qualities. It can likewise be seen that there are one of a kind identifiers for each record in the' Opportunity Number' segment.

Correspondingly, to show select records from the base of the table, the "tail () as sales data. tail ()" can be utilized.

To see the various information types accessible in the informational collection, the Pandas strategy "dtypes () as sales data. dtypes" can be utilized. With this data, the information segments accessible in the information structure can be recorded with their individual information types. We can make sense of, for instance, that the segment "Supplies Subgroup" is an "object" information type and that the segment "Customer Size by Revenue" is a "whole number information type." So, we have a comprehension of segments that either contain number qualities or string information.

Data Visualization

Now, we are through with fundamental information investigation steps, so we won't endeavor to manufacture some engaging plots to depict the data outwardly and find other covered stories from our informational collection.

Of all the accessible Python libraries giving information representation highlights, "Seaborn" is outstanding amongst other accessible choices, so we will utilize the equivalent. Ensure that python plots module gave via "Seaborn" has been introduced on your framework and fit to be utilized. Presently follow the means underneath create wanted plot for the informational collection:

Stage 1 - Import the "Seaborn" module with order "import seaborn as sns".

Stage 2 - Import the "Matplotlib" module with order "import matplotlib. pyplot as plt".

Stage 3 - To set the "foundation shading" of the plot as white, use order "sns.set (style="whitegrid", color-codes=True)".

Stage 4 - To set the "plot size" for all plots, use order "sns.set(arc= {'figure. fig size':(11.7,8.27)})".

Stage 5 – To create a "count plot", use order "sns. count plot ('Route to Market', data=sales_data,hue – 'Opportunity Result')".

Stage 6 – To expel the top and base edges, use order "sns.despine(offset=10, trim=True)".

Stage 7 – To show the plot, , use order "plotplt.show()".

Fast recap - The "Seaborn" and "Matplotlib" modules were imported first. At that point the "set ()" method was utilized to characterize the unmistakable attributes for our plot, for example, plot style and shading. The foundation of the plot was characterized to be white utilizing the code piece "sns.set (style= "whitegrid," shading codes= True)." Then the plot size was characterize utilizing order "sns.set(rc={'figure.figsize':(11.7,8.27)})" that characterize the size of the plot as "11.7px and 8.27px".

Next the order "sns. countplot ('Route To Market', data= deals information, hue='Opportunity Result')" was utilized to create the plot. The "count plot()" method empowers production of a check plot, which can open various contentions to modify the tally plot as per our prerequisites. As a feature of the first "count plot ()" contention, the X-hub was characterized as the section "Course to Market" from the informational collection. The following contention concerns the wellspring of the informational index, which would be "sales data" information system we imported before. The third contention is the shade of the structured presentations that was characterized as "blue" for the section named "won" and "green" for the segment named "misfortune."

Data Pre-Processing

From the information investigation step, we set up that, larger part of the sections in our informational collection are "string information," however "Scikit-Learn" can just process numerical information. Luckily, the Scikit-Learn library offers us numerous approaches to change over string information into numerical information, for instance, "Label Encoder()" procedure. To change straight out names from the informational index, for example, "won" and "misfortune" into numerical qualities, we will utilize the "Label Encoder()" method.

The principal picture contains one section named "shading" with three records to be specific, "Red," "Green" and "Blue." Using the "Label Encoder()" strategy, the record in the equivalent "shading" segment can be changed over to numerical qualities, as appeared in the subsequent picture.

We should start the genuine procedure of transformation now. Utilizing the "flt change()" strategy given by "Label Encoder()," the names in the downright segment like "Course To Market" can be encoded and changed over to numerical names practically identical to those appeared in the outlines above. The capacity "fit change()" requires input marks recognized by the client and thusly Will result in encoded names.

To know how the encoding is cultivated, how about we experience a model rapidly. The code occasion beneath comprises string information as a rundown of urban communities, for example, ["paris," "paris," "tokyo," "amsterdam"] that will be encoded into something equivalent to "[2, 2, 1,3]".

Stage 1 - To import the necessary module, use order "from sklearn import preprocessing."

Stage 2 - To make the Label encoder object, use order "le = preprocessing.LabelEncoder()".

Stage 3 - To change over the unmitigated sections into numerical qualities, use order:

"encoded_value = le.fit_transform(["paris", "paris", "tokyo", "amsterdam"])"

"print(encoded_value) [1 1 2 0]"

What's more, there you have it! We simply changed over our string information names into numerical qualities. The initial step was bringing in the preprocessing module that offers the "Label Encoder()" strategy. Followed by

CHAPTER - 4
DATA SCIENTIST: THE SEXIEST JOB IN THE 21ST CENTURY

The funny thing is that this great value of the data contrasts with that precisely the data is the most abundant resource on the planet (it is estimated that 2.5 trillion bytes of new information is created per day). They don't seem easy to make things compatible. How is it possible that something so abundant is so valuable? Even if it was pure supply and demand, accumulating data should be trivial. And it is, the complex thing is to process them.

Until relatively recently we simply couldn't do it. At the end of the 90s, the field of machine learning began to take on an autonomous entity, our ability to work with immense amounts of data was reduced and the social irruption of the internet did the rest. For a few years we have faced the first great 'democratization' of these techniques. And with that, the boom of data scientists: nobody wants to have an untapped gold mine.

In search of a data scientist

The problem is that, suddenly, there has been a great demand for a profile that until now practically did not exist. Remember that you need statistical knowledge that a programmer does not usually have and computer knowledge that a statistician does not usually even imagine.

Most of the time it has been solved with self-taught training that completes the basic skills that the training program should have but does not have. That is why, today, we can find a great diversity of professional profiles in the world of data science. According to Burtch Works , 32% of active data scientists come from the world of mathematics and statistics, 19% from computer engineering and 16% from other engineering.

How to train?

Degrees:

Today, there are some double degrees in computer engineering and mathematics (Autonomous University of Madrid, Granada, Polytechnic University of Madrid, Polytechnic University of Catalonia, Complutense, Murcia Autonomous University of Barcelona) or in computer science and statistics (University of Valladolid) that seem the best option if we consider this specialization.

Postgraduate

The postgraduate is a very diverse world. We can find postgraduate, masters or specialization courses in almost all universities and a truly excessive private offer. To give some examples we have postgraduate degrees at the UGR, the UAB , the UAM , the UPM or the Pompeu Fabra. However, in postgraduate courses it is more difficult to recommend a specific course.

We must not forget that most of the work of data scientists is in companies that seek to make their databases profitable, because what market orientation is highly recommended. In fact, many of the masters in 'big data'

are offered by business schools such as OEI or Instituto Empresa.

MOOCS

One of the most interesting resources you can find are the moocs (you know, the massive open online courses). In fact recently, we saw that this self-training option could have a lot of future. Starting with the specialization program in Big Data of Coursera, we can find online courses from the best universities in the world. All this without mentioning the numerous tools to learn languages like Python or R.

What languages should be learned?

In reality, as any initiate knows, in programming the choice of one language or another is always complicated. In this election they intervene from technical or formative factors to simple personal preferences. What is clear is that there are some languages more popular than others.

Although common sense tells us that each language is better for certain things, in practice there is a certain rivalry . Personally, I use R but I usually recommend Python. Not only because it is prettier, but because it is multipurpose and that is always an advantage.

Other tools

A fireproof

- Excel: It is not a language and usually does not like those who work with professional data. Or so they say when asked why polls say otherwise: 59% percent of respondents routinely use excel. So, finally, the application of Office spreadsheets is still a lot of war.

The corporate brother and other languages and programs

- Some languages or environments enjoy some success driven by corporate inertia: it is the case of the classic Matlab but progressively it is losing weight and use up to only 6%.

- If we examine the surveys we can find many more languages that obey more particular needs of the practice of data scientists (or the programs they use): Scala (17%), Slack (10%), Perl (12%), C # (6%), Mahout (3%), Apache Hadoop (13%) or Java (23%).

- Also, although it is possible that we should talk about them separately, there are many specific programs (free or proprietary) that are used in data science with different uses. For example, we could talk about Tableau, RapidMiner or Weka.

The labor market: salaries and opportunities

Salaries, as in general in the world of software development, change a lot depending on the place, the

functions and the employer. However, right now it is a well-paid expertise. On a general level and according to the annual KdNuggets survey, salaries / incomes average $ 141,000 for freelancers, 107,000 for employees, 90,000 for government workers or in the non-profit sector; 70,000 dollars for work in universities.

However, these average salaries must be taken with great caution. While the average salary in the United States is between $ 103,000 and $ 131,000, in Western Europe it is between $ 54,000 and $ 82,000. In Spain, we are in similar numbers because, despite our (increasingly smaller) deficit of product companies, we have large companies (especially banks) that have turned in this field.

What differentiates data science from the rest of the development world is perhaps the shortage of professionals. This phenomenon makes salaries relatively inflated and, as more dater profiles appear, they adjust. Therefore, it can be said that it is time to get on the wave of data science.

CHAPTER - 5
USING METHODS

String literals are usually surrounded by single quotation marks and double quotation marks. For example, the world expression 'string' is written in the same way as "string." You can print it in the shell with the print() function, just like I did with the data types in Python shell. The first step is to assign a string to some

variable of your choice. You can write down the name of the variable that you want to use, which can be followed by the equal sign and then the string. Please note that you can use either a single alphabet or a full name as the name of a variable. Use them wisely in a program so that when you read the code, you know the job of each variable.

```
>>> myString = "I am learning deep learning with python."
>>> print(myString)
I am learning deep learning with python.
>>> myString = "I am studying deep learning with python."
>>> print(myString)
I am studying deep learning with python.
>>> myString = """I am studying deep learning,
with Python,
and I am really enjoying it,
and writing programs with it."""
>>> print(myString)
I am studying deep learning,
with Python,
```

```
and I am really enjoying it,

and writing programs with it.

>>> myString = "'I am studying deep learning,

with Python,

and I am really enjoying it,

and writing programs with it.'"

>>> print(myString)

I am studying deep learning,

with Python,

and I am really enjoying it,

and writing programs with it.

>>>
```

Like many programming languages, Python strings are like byte arrays, which represent Unicode characters. There is no character data type in Python. However, a single character is a string that has a length of 1. You can use square brackets to access elements of the string.

```
>>> myString = """I am studying deep learning,

with Python,
```

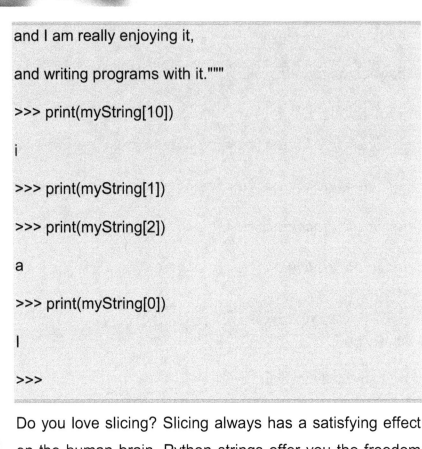

```
and I am really enjoying it,

and writing programs with it."""

>>> print(myString[10])

i

>>> print(myString[1])

>>> print(myString[2])

a

>>> print(myString[0])

I

>>>
```

Do you love slicing? Slicing always has a satisfying effect on the human brain. Python strings offer you the freedom to return a wide range of characters with the help of using the slice syntax. The first step in this regard is to specify the starting index and the ending index. Separate the two by a colon to return a part of the string.

```
>>> myString = """I am studying deep learning,

with Python,

and I am really enjoying it,

and writing programs with it."""
```

```
>>> print(myString[20:35])

earning,

with P

>>> print(myString[10:35])

ing deep learning,

with P

>>> print(myString[0:50])

I am studying deep learning,

with Python,

and I am

>>>
```

Python allows you to slice a string by using negative indexing as well. Let's see how you can do that. The only difference is that you will use negative numbers in the string.

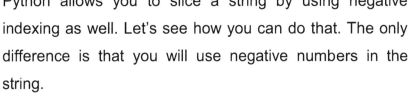

```
>>> myString = """I am studying deep learning,

with Python,

and I am really enjoying it,

and writing programs with it."""
```

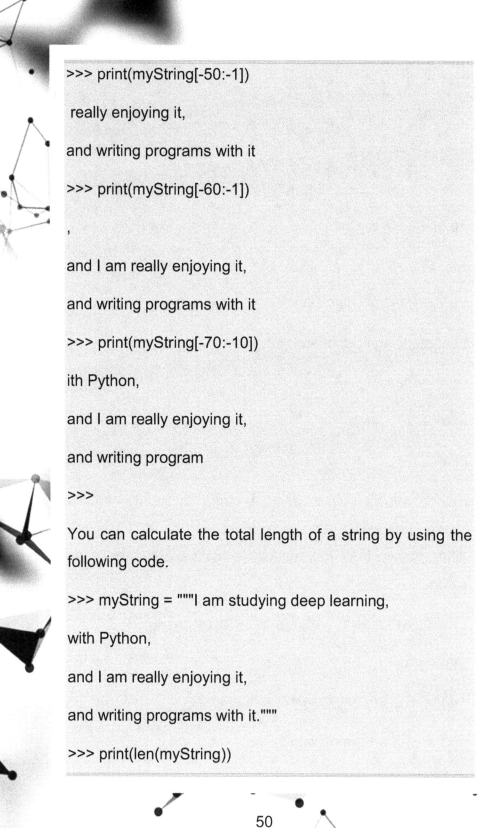

```
>>> print(myString[-50:-1])

 really enjoying it,

and writing programs with it
>>> print(myString[-60:-1])

,

and I am really enjoying it,

and writing programs with it
>>> print(myString[-70:-10])
ith Python,

and I am really enjoying it,

and writing program
>>>
```

You can calculate the total length of a string by using the following code.

```
>>> myString = """I am studying deep learning,

with Python,

and I am really enjoying it,

and writing programs with it."""

>>> print(len(myString))
```

100

>>>

String Methods

The first method that will come under discussion is the strip() method that does the job of removing whitespaces from your string at the start or the end.

```
>>> myString = """ I am studying deep learning,

with Python,

and I am really enjoying it,

and writing programs with it. """
>>> print(myString.strip())
I am studying deep learning,

with Python,

and I am really enjoying it,

and writing programs with it.

>>>
```

In the following example, I will try three different methods on the same string. One method is to convert the text into a lower case; the second is to convert it into the upper case, while the third is to convert the text into title case. All

of them are simple and very handy when you are composing messages that you have to display for your users.

```
>>> myString = """I am studying deep learning,

with Python,

and I am really enjoying it,

and writing programs with it."""

>>> print(myString.lower())

i am studying deep learning,

with python,

and i am really enjoying it,

and writing programs with it.

>>> print(myString.upper())

I AM STUDYING DEEP LEARNING,

WITH PYTHON,

AND I AM REALLY ENJOYING IT,

AND WRITING PROGRAMS WITH IT.

>>> print (myString.title())

I Am Studying Deep Learning,
```

With Python,

And I Am Really Enjoying It,

And Writing Programs with It.

>>>

Let's talk about some more string methods to learn how it operates.

```
>>> myString = """I am studying deep learning,

with Python,

and I am really enjoying it,

and writing programs with it."""
>>> print(myString.replace("studying", "reading"))
```

I am reading deep learning,

with Python,

and I am really enjoying it,

and writing programs with it.

```
>>> print(myString.replace("really", " "))
```

I am studying deep learning,

with Python,

and I am   enjoying it,

and writing programs with it.

```
>>> print(myString.replace("really", ""))
I am studying deep learning,

with Python,

and I am  enjoying it,

and writing programs with it.
>>> print(myString.replace("studying",""))
I am  deep learning,

with Python,

and I am really enjoying it,

and writing programs with it.
>>>
```

In the above example, I attempted to replace a word with a new word. Then I moved on to eliminating a word by replacing it with no word. I tried it thrice to explain how you can manage extra whitespaces that are likely to happen if you don't fix them. The best method is to eliminate extra spaces from the code. There is a special method known as the split() method that can split the string into several substrings.

```
>>> myString = """I am studying deep learning,

with Python,

and I am really enjoying it,

and writing programs with it."""
>>> print(myString.split(","))

['I am studying deep learning,' '\nwith Python,' '\nand I am
really enjoying it,' '\nand writing programs with it.']

>>> myString = "I, am, studying, deep, learning."
>>> print(myString.split(","))

['I', ' am', ' studying', ' deep', ' learning.']

>>>
```

There is another interesting method using which you can check if a certain phrase or a character exists in a particular string or not. There are two keywords 'in' or 'not in' that you can use for this method.

```
>>> myString = "I am studying deep learning."

>>> a = "studying" not in myString

>>> print(a)

False

>>> a = "studying" in myString
```

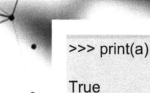

```
>>> print(a)

True

>>>
```

If you can recall the data types that I have shared with you earlier on, you will realize that Python is communicating with you in the Boolean data type. You have got the answer in False and True to your query. This method is the way to extract more information about a Python string through a specific method.

If you have got two strings, you can combine them easily by using the Python string concatenation method. The primary operator that you can use here is the '+' operator. Let's see how to do that.

```
>>> myString = "I am studying deep learning."

>>> myString1 = "with Python."

>>> combstring = myString + myString1

>>> print(combstring)

I am studying deep learning with Python.

>>> myString = "I am studying deep learning."

>>> myString1 = " with Python."

>>> combstring = myString + myString1
```

```
>>> print(combstring)

I am studying deep learning with Python.

>>>
```

The above code snippet has two similar code examples. The first one has a flaw. There is no whitespace in the first after the word learning. Two words have been wrongly combined. I fixed the issue by adding whitespace at the start of the second string. This formula will be helpful for you when you are combining two strings for writing a program. This method is the easiest; however, there is another method that you can use to add necessary space between two strings. Both play the same role, so it is up to you which one you like the most.

```
>>> myString = "I am studying deep learning."

>>> myString1 = "with Python."

>>> combString = myString + " " + myString1

>>> print(combString)

I am studying deep learning with Python.

>>>
```

You can format your string at will by the following method. Formatting a string means that you can combine two data types when you are writing a program for a user. If you try to concatenate them by using the same technique that we used for two strings, this is unlikely to work for you. Let's see what happens when you try to do that.

```
>>> myString = 23
>>> myString1 = "I am John and I am " + myString
Traceback (most recent call last):
  File "<pyshell#98>", line 1, in <module>
    myString1 = "I am John and I am " + myString
TypeError: can only concatenate str (not "int") to str
```

Don't worry. There is a special method for this purpose, the format() method. This method picks up the passed arguments, formats them, and then adds them to the string where you put in the placeholders {}. Let's see how to insert numbers.

```
>>> myString = 23
>>> myString1 = "I am John and I am {}"
>>> print(myString1.format(myString))
I am John and I am 23
```

CHAPTER - 6
MACHINE LEARNING

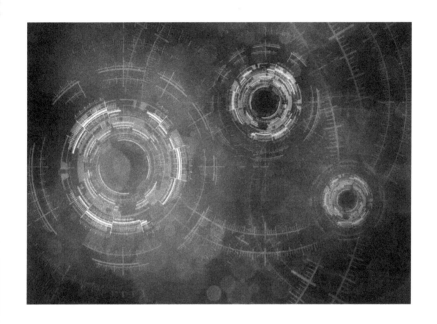

This is going to be an essential part of our data analysis because it helps us to work with some of the algorithms and the models that we want to control in this process. With the help of machine learning and the use of the Python language that we talked about earlier, we are able to see our algorithms actually work and do some of the insights and predictions that we want to work with along the way.

To help us see why machine learning can be useful to our data analysis, we need to take a closer look at how machine learning is going to work in the first place.

What is Machine Learning?

The first thing that we need to take a look at here is the basics of machine learning. This is one of the approaches that we can use with data analytics that will help teach a computer how to learn and react on their own, without the interaction of the programmer. Many of the actions that we will train the system to do will be similar to actions that already come naturally to humans, such as learning from experience.

The algorithms that come with machine learning are going to be able to use computational methods in order to learn information right from the data, without having to rely on an equation that is predetermined as its model. The algorithms are going to adaptively improve some of their own performance as the number of samples that we will use for learning will increase.

With the rise in big data that is available for all industries to use, we will find that machine learning is going to become one of the big techniques that are used to solve a ton of problems in many areas, including the following:

1. Computational finance: This is going to include algorithmic trading, credit scoring, and fraud detection.

2. Computer vision and other parts of image processing. This can be used in some different parts like object detection, motion detection, and face recognition.

3. Computational biology. This is going to be used for a lot of different parts, including DNA sequencing, drug discovery, and tumor detection.

4. Energy production. This can be used to help with a few different actions like load forecasting and to help predict what the prices will be.

5. Manufacturing, aerospace, and automotive options. This is going to be a great technique to work with when it comes to helping with many parts, including predictive maintenance.

6. Natural language processing: This is going to be the way that we can use machine learning to help with applications of voice recognition.

Machine learning and the algorithms that they control are going to work by finding some natural patterns in the data that you can use, including using it in a manner that will help us to make some better predictions and decisions along the way. They are going to be used on a daily basis by businesses and a lot of different companies in order to make lots of critical decisions.

For example, medical facilities can use this to help them to help diagnose patients. And we will find that there are a lot of media sites that will rely on machine learning in order to sift through the potential of millions of options in order to give recommendations to the users.

There are many reasons that your business is able to consider using machine learning. For example, it is going to be useful if you are working with a task that is complex or one that is going to involve a larger amount of data and a ton of variables, but there isn't an equation or a formula that is out there right now to handle it. For example, some of the times when we want to work with machine learning include:

1. Equations and rules that are hand-written and too complex to work with. This could include some options like speech recognition and face recognition.

2. When you find that the rules that are going to change all of the time. This could be seen in actions lie fraud detection from a large number of transactional records.

3. ou find that the nature of your data is going to change on a constant basis, and the program has to be able to adapt along the way. This could be seen when we work

with predicting the trends during shopping when doing energy demand forecasting and even automated trading, to name a few.

Machine learning is more complex, but we are able to combine it together with Python in order to get some amazing results in the process and to ensure that our data analysis is going to work the way that we want.

How Does Machine Learning Work with Data Analysis?

Now that we understand more about how machine learning works and why it is important, it is time for us to take a look more specifically at how machine learning is able to come in and help us out with our data analysis. There are so many reasons why we are able to use machine learning when it comes to the data analysis, so it is important to take some time to look at how we can use it as well.

Machine learning is basically going to be the underlying process for all of the algorithms that we want to create along the way. No matter how simple or how complex your algorithm will be, a lot of the coding and the mechanics that come with it are going to really be run by the machine learning that we will talk about in this guidebook. And with the help of Python, you can make some really amazing algorithms that help us to sort through the data.

So, if you are actually hoping to go through this process of data analysis with the goal to sort through your data and understand what is found inside of it, then you need to learn a bit about machine learning ahead of time. The good news of this is that machine learning will be able to work well with the Python language we talked about above, making sure we can do it with a simple coding language, even if the ideas that derive from machine learning will be overall more complex.

Supervised Machine Learning

The first type of learning that we need to take a look at here is known as supervised machine learning. This is going to be the most basic form of machine learning that we are able to work with, but it will provide us with some of the different parts that we need in order to keep things going well and can help us to train our algorithms in a quick and efficient manner.

To start, supervised learning is simply going to be the process of helping an algorithm to learn to map an input to a particular output. We are going to spend or time on this one while showing lots of examples, with the corresponding answers, to the algorithm in the hopes that it will find the connections and learn. Then, when the training is done, the algorithm will be able to look at new inputs, without the corresponding output, and give us the right answer on its own.

This whole process is going to be achieved when we work on a labeled data set that was collected earlier. If the mapping is done correctly, the algorithm is going to be able to learn in a successful manner. If it is not reaching the goals here, then that means we have to go through and make some changes to our algorithm to help it learn well. Supervised machine learning algorithms, when they are trained well, will be able to make some good predictions for the new data they get later on in the future.

This is going to be a similar process that we would see with a teacher to student scenario. There is going to be a teacher who is able to guide the student to learn well from books and other materials. The student is then going to be tested and, if they are correct, then the student will pass. If not, then the teacher will change things up and will help the student to learn better, so that they are able to learn from the mistakes that they made in the past so that they get better. This is going to be the basics that come with using supervised machine learning.

Unsupervised Machine Learning

The second type of machine learning that we are able to work with is known as unsupervised learning. This is going to be a method that we can use in data analysis because it will enable the machines to go through and classify both the tangible and intangible objects, without having to go through and provide the machine or the system with any information about of time about the objects.

The things or the objects that our machines are going to need to classify are going to be varied, such as the purchasing behaviors of the customer, some of the patterns of behavior of bacteria, and even things like hacker attacks or fraud happening with a bank. The main idea that we are going to be able to see with this kind of learning is that we want to expose our machines to large volumes of data that are varied and then allowing the algorithm to takes time to learn and infer from the data. However, we need to be able to take the time in order to teach the program how it can learn from that data.

CHAPTER - 7
PYTHON

What is Python, why learn Python?

First, Python is a high-level multi-purpose interpreted language. It is well established and focuses on code readability and ease of use. Furthermore, there are innumerable packages and libraries available for Python, from scientific ones to big data specific. All these libraries, combined with Python's easy learning curve, make this language an incredible tool with great versatility.

Some examples of packages related to Data Analysis and Machine Learning presented in include:

Python
Numpy
Pandas
Scipy
Matplotlib
Seaborn
Bokeh
Scikit-Learn
TensorFlow
Pytorch

These are some of the packages, but many others could be listed.

Additionally, according to Stack Overflow, Python has the largest number of questions when compared to the other major programming languages. This can be shown in the graph below.

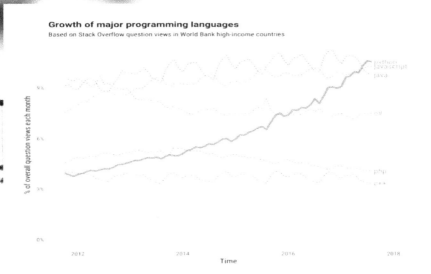

Growth of major programming languages
Based on Stack Overflow question views in World Bank high-income countries

The graph also shows how rapidly this growth happened throughout the years, and that this trend is not slowing down. Therefore, Python is the appropriate language for this book. The version of Python used and referred to in this book is Python 3 because Python 2 is deprecated and soon will not be supported.

Setting Up

1. There are three main ways to download and install Python 3.

   Official Python Website: This installation method is the most common and fastest. However, if you install Python this way, each external library and packages will have to be installed separately. *Therefore, this method is not recommended.*

2. <u>Miniconda</u>: This installer contains the conda package manager and Python. Once installed, you can use the Anaconda Prompt to install other packages and create environments.

3. <u>Anaconda Distribution</u>: This method includes all the packages used in this book and many others. Therefore, this is the recommended installation process. The downside of this installation is that it requires a large file to be downloaded that may not be ideal, depending on your internet speed and bandwidth restrictions.

In all cases, you should download version 3 of Python, which the most current version and is already widely used and supported by third-party libraries.

Please keep in mind that only one installation process is necessary. You should choose the one that is most adequate for you based on their description above. In general, options 1 and 2 are more appropriate for slow/limited internet connections or low disk space, and option 3 is ideal if there are no internet/ storage restrictions.

Below, there is a small step-by-step installation guide for all the options cited previously.

Download Python from the Official Website

1. On the downloads page of the official Python website https://www.python.org/downloads/, your operating system should be automatically detected and the download option available.

2. If your Operational System is correct, just click on the Download Python Button. Otherwise, select one OS in the options below.

3. After clicking, your download should start right away.

Miniconda

Miniconda

	Windows	Mac OS X	Linux
Python 3.7	64-bit (exe installer)	64-bit (bash installer)	64-bit (bash installer)
	32-bit (exe installer)	64-bit (.pkg installer)	32-bit (bash installer)
Python 2.7	64-bit (exe installer)	64-bit (bash installer)	64-bit (bash installer)
	32-bit (exe installer)	64-bit (.pkg installer)	32-bit (bash installer)

Choose the appropriate OS on the following URL https://docs.conda.io/en/latest/miniconda.html and click on the download button. As always, the download should start, and you can proceed to follow the installation process.

Anaconda Distribution

Anaconda 2018.12 for Windows Installer

Python 3.7 version	Python 2.7 version

1. The download section of the Anaconda Distribution for all operating systems is available at https://www.anaconda.com/distribution/#download-section, select your OS.

2. Click Download for version 3, and the download should start right away. Run the installer after the download is completed, and follow the instructions.

Dictionaries

Dictionaries are a powerful data type present in python. It can store indexed values like lists, but the indexes are not a range of integers. Instead, they are unique keys. Therefore, dictionaries are a set of *key: value* pairs. Like sets, dictionaries are not ordered. The keys can be any immutable objects such as strings, tuples, integers, or float numbers.

Defining Dictionaries

Curly brackets and colon are used in an explicit dictionary definition.

```
PYTHON REPL:
>>> a = {}                       # Empty dictionary
>>> a = dict()                   # Empty dictionary
>>> b = {1: 1, 2: 2, 3:3}        # Explicit definitions
>>> c = {42:2, «hi»: 1}
>>> d = {«A»:[1,2,3], «B»: 2}
>>> e = dict(k1=1, k22)          # Considered as string keys
```

Assigning Values to Keys

After a dictionary is created, you can assign values indexing by keys.

```
PYTHON REPL:
>>> d = {}                       # Empty dict
>>> d["a"] = [1, 2]              # Assigning list to key "a"
>>> d[2] = "Hello"              # Assigning string to key 2
>>> d
{'a': [1, 2], 2: 'Hello'}
>>> d[2] = «123»                 # Overriding value in key 2
>>> d
{'a': [1, 2], 2: '123'}
>>> d[«b»]                       # Access invalid key
KeyError: 'b'
```

Get Keys and Values

Dictionary has the built-in methods keys and values to achieve the current values stored.

```
PYTHON REPL:
>>> d = {'a': [1, 2], 2: '123'}       # Same of previous
example
>>> d.keys()                          # List current keys
dict_keys(['a', 2])
>>> d.values()                        # List current values
dict_values([[1, 2], '123'])
```

OBS.: Remember that dictionaries are not an ordered object. Therefore, do not expect order in its keys or values, even though they maintain the insertion order in the latest Python version.

Dictionaries in Loops

In general, you want to know the key: value pairs on a dictionary when iterating. The items method returns both values when used in for loops.

```
INPUT
# Nested Conditions
d = dict(a=1, b=2, c=3)
for k, v in d.items():
print(k)
    print(v)
```
```
OUTPUT
a
1
b
2
c
3
```

Dictionary Comprehension

Dictionaries can be used as in list comprehension.

```
EXAMPLE - Dict Comprehension
# Dict of cubes(values) of number(key) 1 to 4
dc = {x: x ** 3 for x in range(1, 5) }
print(dc)
```
```
OUTPUT
{1: 1, 2: 8, 3: 27, 4: 64}
```

Functions

We already used multiple functions that are built in the
Python programming language, such as print, len, or type.
Generally, a function is defined to represent a set of
instructions that will be repeatedly called. In order to
achieve the desired task, a function may or may not need
multiple inputs, called arguments.

```
EXAMPLE - Built-in Functions
a = [1, 2, 3]
s = len(a)      # variable a is the argument of function len
print(s)        # variable s is the argument of function
print
OUTPUT
3
```

Not all functions need an argument, for example, the built-in function help.

```
EXAMPLE - Built-in Functions
help()               # no values is passed as argument
OUTPUT
Welcome to Python 3.6's help utility!
...
```

Testing your Code

In a Python programming language, there are several technique methods that are used in testing a particular kind of code. Let us venture into the actual methods that are normally involved:

Automated versus manual testing.

Exploratory testing is a type of manual testing that is committed without a specific plan, where a developer is just trying to explore the actual application. In a bid to complete certain amounts of manual tests, a developer is obligated to draft a list of all the available features that a certain application contains, the various kinds of inputs that are normally accepted, and the possible expected results. With this, the developer is expected to go back to his or her list whenever changes are made to a particular set of programs, an activity that is so much tiresome and unsatisfying. It is at this point where automated testing comes in.

Automated testing is the execution of the set program of code by a script in place of a particular human. Python language comes in handy is a set of tools and certain libraries that aids a particular developer in making automated testing to its application.

Unit tests versus integration tests.

A unit test is basically a kind of smaller test that checks whether a single component in a particular program works the right way so as to make it functional, whereas an integration test is the type of testing that ensures all the components that are involved in a particular set of program work well with each other. Both unit tests and integration tests can be written in a specific program.

Test runners are basically tools that pick up the source code directory of a particular kind of program that contains unit tests and various settings, gets to execute them, and eventually outputs the results to the log files or the console.

Every program has certain data that allows it to function and operate in the way we want. The data can be a text, a number, or any other thing in between.

Whether complex or as simple as you like, these data types are the cogs in a machine that allow the rest of the mechanism to connect and work.

Python is a host to a few data types and, unlike its competitors, it does not deal with an extensive range of things.

That is good because we have less to worry about and yet achieve accurate results despite the lapse.

Python was created to make our lives, as programmers, a lot easier.

Numeric Data Type

Just as the number suggests, Python is able to recognize numbers rather well.

The numbers are divided into two pairs:

- Integer – A positive and/or negative whole numbers that are represented without any decimal points.
- Float – A real number that has a decimal point representation.

This means, if you were to use 100 and 100.00, one would be identified as an integer while the other will be deemed as a float.

So why do we need to use two various number representations?

If you are designing a program, suppose a small game that has a character's life of 10, you might wish to keep the

program in a way that whenever a said character takes a hit, his life reduces by one or two points.

However, to make things a little more precise, you may need to use float numbers.

Now, each hit might vary and may take 1.5, 2.1, or 1.8 points away from the life total.

Using floats allows us to use greater precision, especially when calculations are on the cards.

If you aren't too troubled about the accuracy, or your programming involves whole numbers only, stick to integers.

Booleans

Ah! The one with the funny name.

Boolean (or bool) is a data type that can only operate on and return two values: True or False.

Booleans are a vital part of any program, except the ones where you may never need them, such as our first program.

These are what allow programs to take various paths if the result is true or false.

Here's a little example.

Suppose you are traveling to a country you have never been to.

There are two choices you are most likely to face.

If it is cold, you will be packing your winter clothes.

If it is warm, you will be packing clothes which are appropriate for warm weather.

Simple, right?

That is exactly how the Booleans work.

We will look into the coding aspect of it as well.

For now, just remember, when it comes to true and false, you are dealing with a bool value.

List

While this is slightly more advanced for someone at this stage of learning, the list is a data type that does what it sounds like.

It lists objects, values, or stores data within square brackets ([]).

Here's what a list would look like:

```
month = ['Jan', 'Feb', 'March', 'And so on!']
```

We will be looking into this separately, where we will discuss lists, tuples, and dictionaries.

Surely, they are used within Python, but how?

If you think you can type in the numbers and true and false, all on their own, it will never work.

Variables

You have the passengers, but you do not have a mode of commuting; they will have nowhere to go.

These passengers would just be folks standing around, waiting for some kind of transportation to pick them up.

Similarly, data types cannot function alone.

They need to be 'stored' in these vehicles, which can take them places.

These special vehicles, or as we programmers refer to as containers, are called 'variables,' and they are the elements that perform the magic for us.

Variables are specialized containers that store a specific value in them and can then be accessed, called, modified, or even removed when the need arises.

Every variable that you may create will hold a specific type of data in them.

You cannot add more than one type of data within a variable.

In other programming languages, you will find that in order to create a variable, you need to use the keyword 'var' followed by an equals mark '=' and then the value.

In Python, it is a lot easier, as shown below:

```
name = "John"

age = 33

weight = 131.50

is_married = True
```

In the above, we have created a variable named 'name' and given it a value of characters.

If you recall strings, we have used double quotation marks to let the program know that this is a string.

We then created a variable called age.

Here, we simply wrote 33, which is an integer as there are no decimal figures following that.

You do not need to use quotation marks here at all.

Next, we created a variable 'weight' and assigned it a float value.

Finally, we created a variable called 'is_married' and assigned it a 'True' bool value.

If you were to change the 'T' to 't', the system will not recognize it as a bool and will end up giving an error.

Focus on how we used the naming convention for the last variable.

We will be ensuring that our variables follow the same naming convention.

You can even create blank variables if you feel like you may need these at a later point in time, or wish to initiate them at no value at the start of the application.

For variables with numeric values, you can create a variable with a name of your choosing and assign it a value of zero.

Alternatively, you can create an empty string as well by using opening and closing quotation marks only.

```
empty_variable1 = 0

empty_variable2 = ""
```

You do not have to necessarily name them like this, you can come up with more meaningful names so that you and any other programmer who may read your code would understand.

I have given them these names to ensure anyone can immediately understand their purpose.

Now we have learned how to create variables, let's learn how to call them.

What's the point of having these variables if we are never going to use them, right?

Let's create a new set of variables.

Have a look here:

```
name = "James"

age = 43

height_in_cm = 163

occupation = "Programmer"
```

I do encourage you to use your own values and play around with variables if you like.

In order for us to call the name variable, we simply need to type the name of the variable.

In order to print that to the console, we will do this:

```
print(name)

Output

James
```

The same goes for the age, the height variable, and occupation.

But what if we wanted to print them together and not separately?

Try running the code below and see what happens:

```
print(name age height_in_cm occupation)
```

Surprised? Did you end up with this?

```
print(name age height_in_cm occupation)
        ^
```

SyntaxError: invalid syntax

Process finished with exit code 1

Here is the reason why that happened.

When you were using a single variable, the program knew what variable that was.

The minute you added a second, a third, and a fourth variable, it tried to look for something that was written in that manner.

Since there wasn't any, it returned with an error that otherwise says:

"Umm… Are you sure, Sir? I tried looking everywhere, but I couldn't find this 'name age height_in_cm occupation' element anywhere."

All you need to do is add a comma to act as a separator like so:

```
print(name, age, height_in_cm, occupation)

Output:

James 43 163 Programmer
```

"Your variables, Sir!"

And now, it knew what we were talking about.

The system recalled these variables and was successfully able to show us what their values were.

But what happens if you try to add two strings together?

What if you wish to merge two separate strings and create a third-string as a result?

```
first_name = "John"

last_name = "Wick"
```

To join these two strings into one, we can use the '+' sign.

The resulting string will now be called a String Object, and since this is Python we are dealing with, everything within this language is considered as an object.

```
first_name = "John"

last_name = "Wick"

first_name + last_name
```

Here, we did not ask the program to print the two strings.

If you wish to print these two instead, simply add the print function and type in the string variables with a + sign in the middle within parentheses.

Sounds good, but the result will not be quite what you expect:

```
first_name = "John"

last_name = "Wick"

print(first_name + last_name)

Output:

JohnWick
```

Hmm. Why do you think that happened?

Certainly, we did use a space between the two variables.

The problem is that the two strings have combined together, quite literally here, and we did not provide a white space (blank space) after John or before Wick; it will not include that.

Even the white space can be a part of a string.

To test it out, add one character of space within the first line of code by tapping on the friendly spacebar after John.

Now try running the same command again, and you should see "John Wick" as your result.

The process of merging two strings is called concatenation.

While you can concatenate as many strings as you like, you cannot concatenate a string and an integer together.

If you really need to do that, you will need to use another technique to convert the integer into a string first and then concatenate the same.

CHAPTER - 9
OBJECT ORIENTED PROGRAMMING
IN PYTHON

Object and Class in Python

Python supports different programming approaches as it is a multi-paradigm. An object in Python has an attribute and behavior.

Example

Car as an object:

Attributes: color, mileage, model, age.

Behavior: reverse, speed, turn, roll, stop, start.

Class

It is a template for creating an object.

Example

class Car:

NOTE:

By convention, we write the class name with the first letter as uppercase. A class name is in singular form by convention.

Syntax
class Name_of_Class:

From a class, we can construct objects by simply making an instance of the class. The class_name() operator creates an object by assigning the object to the empty method.

Object/Class Instantiation
From our class Car, we can have several objects such as a first car, second care or SUVs.

Example

Start IDLE.

Navigate to the File menu and click New Window.

Type the following:

```
my_car=Car()
```

   pass

Practice Exercise

Create a class and an object for students.

Create a class and an object for the hospital.

Create a class and an object for a bank.

Create a class and an object for a police department.

Example

Start IDLE.

Navigate to the File menu and click New Window.

Type the following:

class Car:

category="Personal Automobile"

   def __init__(self, model, insurance):

      self.model = model

```
        self.insurance =insurance

subaru=Car("Subaru","Insured")

toyota=Car("Toyota","Uninsured")

print("Subaru is a {}".format(subaru._class_.car))

print("Toyota is a {}".format(toyota._class_.car))

print("{} is {}".format(subaru.model, subaru.insurance))

print("{} is {}".format(toyota.model, toyota.insurance))
```

Methods

Functions defined within a body of the class are known as methods and are basic functions. Methods define the behaviors of an object.

Example

Start IDLE.

Navigate to the File menu and click New Window.

Type the following:

```
def __init__(self, model, insurance):

    self.model = model

    self.insurance =insurance

  def ignite(self, ignite):
```

```
        return "{} ignites {}".format(self.model, ignition)

    def stop(self):

        return "{} is now stopping".format(self.model)

subaru=Car("Subaru","Insured")

print(subaru.ignite('"Fast"'))

print(subaru.stop())
```

NOTE

The methods ignite() and stop() are referred to as instance methods because they are an instance of the object created.

Practice Exercise

- Create a class Dog and instantiate it.
- Create a Python program to show names of two dogs and their two attributes from a.

Inheritance

A way of creating a new class by using details of existing class devoid of modifying it is called inheritance. The derived class or child class is the newly formed class while the existing class is called parent or base class.

Example

Start IDLE.

Navigate to the File menu and click New Window.

Type the following:

```python
class Dog:

    def __init__(self):

        print("Dog is available")

    def whoisThis(self):

        print("Dog")

    def walk(self):

        print("Walks gently")

class Spitz(Dog):        #Child class

    def __init__(self):

        super().__init__()

        print("Spitz is now available")

    def whoisThis(self):

        print("Pitbull")

    def wag(self):

        print("Strong")

pitbull = Pitbull()
```

```
pitbull.whoisThis()

pitbull.walk()

pitbull.wag()
```

Discussion

We created two Python classes in the program above. The classes were Dog as the base class and Pitbull as the derived class. The derived class inherits the functions of the base class. The method _init_() and the function super() are used to pull the content of _init_() method from the base class into the derived class.

Encapsulation in Python

Encapsulation in Python Object Oriented Programming approach is meant to help prevent data from direct modification. Private attributes in Python are denoted using a single or double underscore as a prefix.

Example

Start IDLE.

Navigate to the File menu and click New Window.

Type the following:

"_" or "_".

class Tv:

```python
    def __init__(self):

        self.__Finalprice = 800

    def offer(self):

        print("Offering Price: {}".format(self.__finalprice))

    def set_final_price(self, offer):

        self.__finalprice = offer

t = Tv()

t.offer()

t.__finalprice = 950

t.offer()

# using setter function

t.setFinalPrice(990)

t.sell()
```

Discussion

The program defined a class Tv and used _init_(0 methods to hold the final offering price of the TV. Along the way, we attempted to change the price but could not manage. The reason for the inability to change is because Python treated the _finalprice as private attributes. The

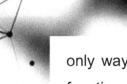

only way to modify this value was through using a setter function, setMaxPrice() that takes price as a parameter.

Object Creation in Python

Example from the previous class

Open the previous program file with class Bright

```
student1=Bright ()
```

Discussion

The last program will create object student1, a new instance. The attributes of objects can be accessed via the specific object name prefix. The attributes can be a method or data including the matching class functions. In other terms, Bright.salute is a function object and student1.salute will be a method object.

Example

Start IDLE.

Navigate to the File menu and click New Window.

Type the following:

class Bright:

  "Another class again!"

  c = 20

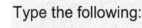

```
    def salute(self):

        print('Hello')

student2 = Bright()

print(Bright.salute)

print(student2.salute)

student2.salute()
```

Discussion

We invoked the student2.salute() despite the parameter 'self' and it still worked without placing arguments. The reason for this phenomenon is because each time an object calls its method, the object itself is passed as the first argument. The implication is that student2.salute() translates into student2.salute(student2). It is the reason for the 'self; name.

Constructors

Start IDLE.

Navigate to the File menu and click New Window.

Type the following:

class NumberComplex

class ComplexNumber:

```
    def __init__(self,realnum = 0,i = 0):

        self.real = realnum

        self.imaginarynum = i

    def getData(self):

        print("{0}+{1}j".format(self.realnumber,self.imaginaryn
um))

complex1 = NumberComplex(2,3)

complex1.getData()

complex2 = NumberComplex(5)

complex2.attribute = 10

print((complex2.realnumber,

complex2.imaginarynumber, complex2.attribute))

complex1.attribute
```

Deleting Objects and Attributes

The del statement is used to delete attributes of an object at any instance.

Example

Start IDLE.

Navigate to the File menu and click New Window.

Type the following:

```
complex1 = NumberComplex(2,3)

del complex1.imaginarynumber

complex1.getData()

del NumberComplex.getData

complex1.getData()
```

Deleting the Entire Object

Example

Start IDLE.

Navigate to the File menu and click New Window.

Type the following:

```
complex1=NumberComplex (1,3)

del complex1
```

Discussion

When complex1=NumberComplex(1,3) is done, a new instance of the object gets generated in memory and the name complex1 ties with it. The object does not immediately get destroyed as it temporarily stays in

memory before the garbage collector purges it from memory. The purging of the object helps free resources bound to the object and enhances system efficiency. Garbage destruction Python refers to automatic destruction of unreferenced objects.

Inheritance in Python

In Python inheritance allows us to specify a class that takes all the functionality from the base class and adds more. It is a powerful feature of OOP.

Syntax

class ParentClass:

   Body of parent class

class ChildClass(ParentClass):

   Body of derived class

Example

Start IDLE.

Navigate to the File menu and click New Window.

Type the following:

class Rect_mine(Rect_mine):

   def __init__(self):

      Shape.__init__(self,4)

```python
def getArea(self):

    s1, s2, s3,s4 = self.count_sides

    perimeter = (s1+s2+s3+s4)

    area = (s1*s2)

    print('The rectangle area is:' %area)
```

Example 2

```python
r = rect_mine()

r.inputSides()

Type b1 : 4

Type l1 : 8

Type b2 : 4

Type l1:    8

r.dispSides()

Typo b1 is 4.0

Type l1 is 8.0

Type b2 is 4.0

Type l1 is 8.0

r.getArea()
```

Method Overriding in Python

When a method is defined in both the base class and the derived class, the method in the child class/derived class will override the parent/base class. In the above example, _init_() method in Rectangle class will override the _init_() in Shape class.

Inheritance in Multiple Form in Python

Example

Start IDLE.

Navigate to the File menu and click New Window.

Type the following:

```
class Parent1:

    pass

class Parent2:

    pass

class MultiInherit(Parent1, Parent2):

    pass
```

In this case, MultiInherit is derived from class Parent1 and Parent2.

Multilevel Inheritance

Inheriting from a derived class is called multilevel inheritance.

Example

Start IDLE.

Navigate to the File menu and click New Window.

Type the following:

```
class Parent:

    pass

class Multilevel1(Parent):

    pass

class Multilevel2(Multilevel1):

    pass
```

Discussion

Multilevel1 derives from Parent, and Multilevel2 derives from Multilevel1.

Method Resolution Order

Example

Start IDLE.

Navigate to the File menu and click New Window.

Type the following:

```
print(issubclass(list,object))

print(isinstance(6.7,object))

print(isinstance("Welcome",object))
```

Discussion

The particular attribute in a class will be scanned first. The search will continue into parent classes. This search does not repeat searching the same class twice. The approach or order of searching is sometimes called linearization of multiderived class in Python. The Method Resolution Order refers to the rules needed to determine this order.

Operator Overloading

Inbuilt classes can use operators and the same operators will behave differently with different types. An example is the + that depending on context will perform concatenation of two strings, arithmetic addition on numbers, or merge lists. Operating overloading is an OOP feature that allows assigning varying meaning to an operator subject to context.

Making Class Compatible with Inbuilt Special Functions

Example

Start IDLE.

Navigate to the File menu and click New Window.

Type the following:

```python
class Planar:

    def __init__(self, x_axis= 0, y_axis = 0):

        self.x_axis = x_axis

        self.y_axis = y_axis

    def __str__(self):

        return "({0},{1})".format(self.x_axis,self.y_axis)
```

Discussion

```python
planar1=Planar(3,5)

print(planar1)          #The output will be (3,5)
```

Using More Inbuilt Methods

Example

Start IDLE.

Navigate to the File menu and click New Window.

Type the following:

```python
class Planar:
```

```
def __init__(self, x_axis= 0, y_axis = 0):

    self.x_axis = x_axis

    self.y_axis = y_axis

str(planar1)

format(planar1)
```

Discussion

It then follows that each time we invoke format(planar1) or str(planar1), Python is in effect executing planar1._str_() thus the name, special functions.

CHAPTER - 10
LEARNING PYTHON FROM SCRATCH

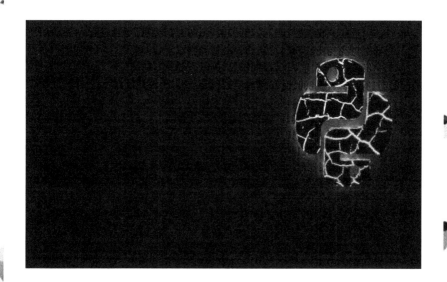

Even before buying this book, you had some idea as to how important and in-demand Python is. We also read a little about it earlier on and saw how it is overtaking many mainstream programming languages. We walked through a step-by-step guide to download Python 3, the integrated development environment, or the text/code editor and set everything up. Lastly, you created your first program: well done!

Now, it is time to stop scratching the surface and dive deep into the world of Python. There are far too many components and aspects to learn about Python, but we will only be focusing on what is essential for anyone to know and learn as a beginner.

Consider this as a grammar for any other language. Without grammar, the language sounds broken, and so does Python.

Python at First Glance

Let us start with the program below:

```
print("I made it!")

print("======")

print("If I only knew it would be this easy")

print("======")

print("I would have taken up Python ages ago")

print("======")
```

We used a print command to have our message printed at the console box as our output of the program. Calling 'print' a command is technically wrong; it is a function. While we will be covering functions and methods in detail later on, for now, just remember that functions are names of commands which are followed by parenthesis "()" where the brackets will either be empty or contain some type of data. There are set parameters that are pre-defined, meaning that certain functions will only be able to accept a specific type of data.

In the above example, we used nothing more than text. A few letters to create a message, and that is it. In Python, things work differently. Text is not identified as text. We need to tell Python that we want this to be printed as text. How do we do that? We use single or double quotation marks, which allows Python to understand that anything within the quotes is text, and it needs to print it the way it is.

I bet you most of you may not have noticed how all of the lines start with a lowercase 'p' instead of the opposite. Ah, yes! Now that you noticed it let me tell you why we did that.

Python is a case-sensitive language. It considers everything as a character, not a letter or text. This means that the lowercase 'p' will not be the same character as the uppercase 'P' and so on, and so forth.

Print

PRINT

print

PrinT

pRINt

All of these will be treated differently by Python, and for printing purposes, these will not work at all except for 'print' as that is the standard way of outputting things.

To name anything in Python, we normally use lowercases for one-word commands. This isn't something that is exclusive to Python, as every language uses some way as standard to write codes. What makes Python different is the sheer amount of thought that was put into the naming convention to make code easier to read. Remember this, anything with more than the word, you can use a few ways to do so as shown here:

last_name

LastName

lastname

LASTNAME

In most of the cases, we will be using the first approach where each letter begins with a lowercase. For components with more than one word, we will be using underscores to separate them. The next in line is generally used only in cases of classes. At this point in time, you do not have to worry about what classes are. Just remember that words with the first letter as capital and that having no underscores is an example of Camel Case, and used for classes.

Next down the line is the way we use to name packages. Here, all the words begin and end with lowercase letters and have no underscores between them. On the polar opposite, we have our last entry, which is used to define constants. Here, all the letters are in uppercase and have no underscores separating the words.

Boring, wasn't it? I know! But it is something you may want to remember as we will be doing quite a lot of these. You should know when to use which convention, as this greatly improves the code readability. The entire point of Python is to promote code readability, and if we go against that, there's not much point in learning Python.

Now that we have covered this let us start by discussing data types that are at work within Python. Without these, no programming language would operate or work. They are what we use as inputs, and these are what direct the program per our desire accordingly.

What Are Data Types?

Every program has certain data that allows it to function and operate in the way we want. The data can be a text, a number, or any other thing in between. Whether complex in nature or as simple as you like, these data types are the cogs in a machine that allow the rest of the mechanism to connect and work.

Python is a host to a few data types and, unlike its competitors, it does not deal with an extensive range of things. That is good because we have less to worry about and yet achieve accurate results despite the lapse. Python was created to make our lives, as programmers, a lot easier.

Strings

In Python, and other programming languages, any text value that we may use, such as names, places, sentences, they are all referred to as strings. A string is a collection of characters, not words or letters, which is marked by the use of single or double quotation marks.

To display a string, use the print command, open up a parenthesis, put in a quotation mark, and write anything. Once done, we generally end the quotation marks and close the bracket.

Since we are using PyCharm, the IntelliSense detects what we are about to do and delivers the rest for us immediately. You may have noticed how it jumped to the rescue when you only type in the opening bracket. It will automatically provide you with a closing one. Similarly, for the quotation marks, one or two, it will provide the closing ones for you. See why we are using PyCharm? It greatly helps us out.

"I do have a question. Why do we use either single or double quotation marks if both provide the same result?"

Ah! Quite the eye. There is a reason we use these, let me explain by using the example below:

```
print('I'm afraid I won't be able to make it')

print("He said "Why do you care?"")
```

Try and run this through PyCharm. Remember, to run, simply click on the green play-like button on the top right side of the interface.

"C:\Users\Programmer\AppData\Local\Programs\Python\Python37-32\python.exe"
"C:/Users/Programmer/PycharmProjects/PFB/Test1.py"

 File
"C:/Users/Programmer/PycharmProjects/PFB/Test1.py",
line 1

```
print('I'm afraid I won't be able to make it')
```

 ^

SyntaxError: invalid syntax

Process finished with exit code 1

Here's a hint: That's an error!

So what happened here? Try and revisit the inputs. See how we started the first print statement with a single quote? Immediately, we ended the quote using another quotation mark. The program only accepted the letter 'I' as a string. You may have noticed how the color may have changed for every other character from 'm' until 'won' after which the program detects yet another quotation mark and accepts the rest as another string. Quite confusing, to be honest.

Similarly, in the second statement, the same thing happened. The program saw double quotes and understood it as a string, right until the point the second instance of double quotation marks arrives. That's where it did not bother checking whether it is a sentence or that it may have still been going on. Computers do not understand English; they understand binary communications. The compiler is what runs when we press the run button. It compiles our code and interprets the same into a series of ones and zeros so that the computer may understand what we are asking it to do.

This is exactly why the second it spots the first quotation mark, it considers it as a start of a string, and ends it immediately when it spots a second quotation mark, even if the sentence was carrying onwards.

To overcome this obstacle, we use a mixture of single and double quotes when we know we need to use one of these within the sentence. Try and replace the opening and closing quotation marks in the first state as double quotation marks on both ends. Likewise, change the quotation marks for the second statement to single quotation marks as shown here:

```
print("I'm afraid I won't be able to make it")

print('He said "Why do you care?"')
```

Now the output should look like this:

I'm afraid I won't be able to make it

He said "Why do you care?"

Lastly, for strings, the naming convention does not apply to the text of the string itself. You can use regular English writing methods and conventions without worries, as long as that is within the quotation marks. Anything outside it will not be a string in the first place, and will or may not work if you change the cases.

Did you know that strings also use triple quotes? Never heard that before, have you? We will cover that shortly!

Numeric Data type

Just as the number suggests, Python is able to recognize numbers rather well. The numbers are divided into two pairs:

- Integer – A positive and/or negative whole numbers that are represented without any decimal points.
- Float – A real number that has a decimal point representation.

This means, if you were to use 100 and 100.00, one would be identified as an integer while the other will be deemed as a float. So why do we need to use two various number representations?

If you are designing a program, suppose a small game that has a character's life of 10, you might wish to keep the program in a way that whenever a said character takes a hit, his life reduces by one or two points. However, to make things a little more precise, you may need to use float numbers. Now, each hit might vary and may take 1.5, 2.1, or 1.8 points away from the life total.

Using floats allows us to use greater precision, especially when calculations are on the cards. If you aren't too troubled about the accuracy, or your programming involves whole numbers only, stick to integers.

CHAPTER - 11
TOP PROGRAMMING LANGUAGES AT TOP COMPANIES AND PYTHON

Python is consistently contrasted and other deciphered dialects, for example, Java, JavaScript, Perl, Tcl, or Smalltalk. Associations with C++, Common Lisp and Scheme can likewise be edifying. Around there, I will rapidly contrast Python and all of these dialects. These examinations center around what every language gives in a manner of speaking. The decision of a programming language is a significant part of the time composed by other legitimate impediments, for instance, cost, accessibility, getting ready, and prior endeavor, or even enthusiastic connection. Since these perspectives are exceptionally factor, it has all the earmarks of being a pointless activity to consider them much for this relationship.

Java

Python programs are usually expected to run more gradually than Java programs, yet they likewise put aside generously less exertion to create. Python programs are normally 3-5 times shorter than indistinguishable Java programs. This distinction can be credited to Python's worked unimportant level data types and its dynamic forming. For example, a Python programming engineer consumes no time pronouncing the sorts of factors or contentions, and Python's amazing polymorphic rundown. Moreover, word reference types, for which rich syntactic help are gotten straight together with the language, discover use in essentially every Python program. Because of the run-time composing, Python's run time must perform progressively intensive contrasted with Java programming language. For example, while assessing the articulation a+b, it ought to at first research the things on a and b to discover their type, which isn't known at compile time. It by then gathers the reasonable expansion activity, which may be an over-burden client characterized technique. Java, on the other hand, can play out a successful number or skimming point expansion, in any case, requires variable assertions for an and b, and doesn't permit over-burdening of the + administrator for events of client characterized classes.

Consequently, Python is an unfathomably improved fit as a "stick" language, while Java is better portrayed as a low-level usage language. Truly, the two together make a splendid blend. Parts can be made in Java and united to shape applications in Python; Python can likewise be utilized to show sections until their game plan can be "solidified" in a Java execution. To assist this with arranging of progress, a Python usage written in Java is a work in progress, which permits calling Python code from Java and the contrary path around. In this use, Python source code is suggested Java bytecode (with assistance from a run-time library to help Python's dynamic semantics).

JavaScript

Python's "object-based" subset is commonly proportionate to JavaScript. Like JavaScript (and not in any manner like Java), Python bolsters a programming style that uses

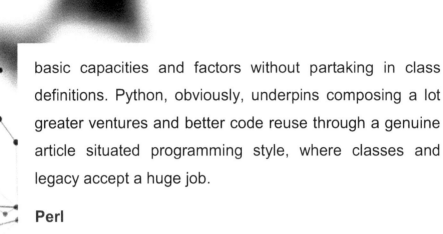

basic capacities and factors without partaking in class definitions. Python, obviously, underpins composing a lot greater ventures and better code reuse through a genuine article situated programming style, where classes and legacy accept a huge job.

Perl

Python and Perl begin from a comparative foundation (UNIX scripting, which both have long grown out of), and sport various comparative highlights, yet have a substitute method of working. Perl accentuates support for fundamental application-situated errands, for instance, by having worked in standard articulations, document filtering and report making highlights. Python accentuates support for ordinary programming strategies, for instance, data structure plan and article arranged programming, and urges programming architects to compose clear (and along these lines practical) code by giving a rich anyway not excessively mysterious documentation. As a result, Python approaches Perl yet rarely beats it in its unique application area; in any case, Python has importance well past Perl's forte.

Tcl

Like Python, Tcl is commonsense as an application development language, just as an autonomous programming language. Notwithstanding, Tcl, which for the most part stores all data as strings, is weak on data structures and executes normal code much more slow than Python. Tcl likewise needs includes required for composing tremendous endeavors, for example, explicit namespaces. All things considered, while a "standard" gigantic application using Tcl usually contains Tcl increases recorded in C or C++ that are obvious to that application, a comparable Python application can much of the time be written in "unadulterated Python". Unadulterated Python improvement is much quicker than to compose and investigate a C or C++ programming language part. It has been said that Tcl's one sparing worth is the Tk toolbox. Python has gotten an interface to Tk as its standard GUI part library.

cl 8.0 keeps an eye on the speed issues by giving a bytecode compiler limited data type backing, besides, it fuses namespaces. In any case, it is uptil now an on a very basic level progressively bulky programming language.

Smalltalk

Perhaps the most noteworthy distinction among Python and Smalltalk is Python's more "standard" grammar, which gives up it a leg on engineer planning. Like Smalltalk, Python has dynamic and obligatory composition, and everything in Python is a thing. Smalltalk's standard library of variety data types is progressively refined, while

Python's library has more workplaces for overseeing Internet and WWW genuine components, for instance, email, HTML and FTP.

Python has an alternate method of working concerning the improved condition and circulation of code. Where Smalltalk by and large has a solid "system picture" which contains both the earth and the client's program, Python stores both standard modules and client modules in particular documents which can without a very remarkable stretch be redone or conveyed outside the structure. One outcome is that there is numerous decision for connecting a Graphical User Interface (GUI) to a Python program since the GUI isn't solidified with the structure.

C++

Practically totally said for Java additionally applies for C++, just more so: where Python code is normally 3-5 times shorter than proportionate Java code, it is much of the time 5-10 times shorter than equivalent C++ code! Story confirmation suggests that one Python programming architect can finish in two months what two C++ engineers can't complete in a year. Python sparkles as a paste language used to consolidate parts written in C++.

Basic Lisp and Scheme

These dialects are close to Python in their dynamic semantics, yet so phenomenal in their way to deal with sentence structure that an examination turns out to be just about a strict contention: is Lisp's absence of grammar a touch of a bit of leeway or a hindrance? It ought to be seen that Python has careful cutoff points like those of Lisp, and Python exercises can create and execute program parts on the fly. Typically, genuine properties are authoritative: Common Lisp is enormous (in each sense), and the Scheme world is partitioned between various contradictory adaptations, where Python has a solitary, free, minimal execution.

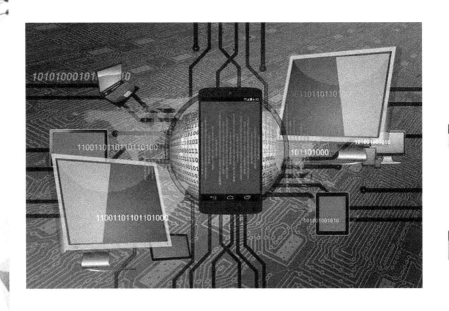

An internet software runs on a far off server as a software program utility. Most of the time, web browsers are for net packages like the net. Some of the packages are used for intranets, schools, firms, and organizations. They are not the same as other applications since you do now not want to put in them. Some of the not unusual net packages consist of Flickr, Wikipedia, Facebook, and Mibbit. They are famous due to the fact that maximum of the running systems is on the net browser and programmers can exchange them with ease.

Several blessings come with the use of internet software:

They do no longer want to be mounted due to the fact they run internal a browser. They do no longer require numerous space for storage handiest a display of facts.

- With internet packages. It helps with compatibility problems; all is wanted is a browser.

- Most of the records used are remotely stored; for this reason, ease of cooperation and communication.

- Web software enables in mail and communication.

Apart from the listed blessings of web packages, there also are drawbacks:

Most of the recognized internet packages will seem to look special in comparison to the normal applications. The purpose is that they run inside a browser. The person experience might be extraordinary and no longer appreciated via many.

To be capable of observing standards, web packages want to be coded, and any small modifications will prevent the internet software from being used in any browser.

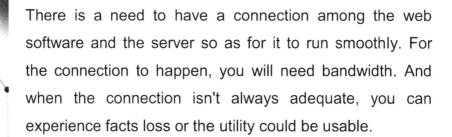

There is a need to have a connection among the web software and the server so as for it to run smoothly. For the connection to happen, you will need bandwidth. And when the connection isn't always adequate, you can experience facts loss or the utility could be usable.

Most of the internet programs rely upon the server that hosts them. When it's far off, the net software isn't always usable, however the conventional applications will still paintings.

The overall control of the net utility is with the mother employer. They have the strength to create a new version while they experience like it.

When the data is remotely stored, exporting it to be used by other programs might be hard.

Web applications permit the organization to track all of the activities of the users, therefore private issues.

At this point, you need to recognize how an internet application works. Most of the internet programs are coded in a language this is browser supported, like HTML or JavaScript. And the foremost purpose is that the languages rely on the browser to be able to execute their programs. You need to recognize that a number of these packages are dynamic, and they'll require server-aspect processing. Others are considered static and will now not want any processing from the server.

When you have an internet software, you will want a webserver to manage all of the requests that the customer has. The server will assist in performing all the obligations and store records and statistics. The software server consists of ASP, PHP, and JSP. A normal web utility has a specific flow:

The user will trigger a request the usage of the internet that is going to the webserver. This may be done through the web browser or consumer interface at the application.

The web server will then ahead that request to the unique web application server.

The asked project might be performed through the internet utility server; this includes querying the database or information processing with the intention to generate the specified results.

The results will be dispatched to the internet server by way of of the net application server; that is in regards to the statistics processed or the specified data.

The client gets a response from the webserver; they'll get the information that they have got requested and it will seem on the user's display.

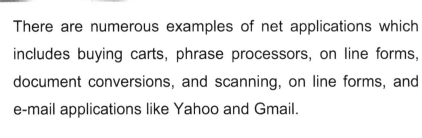

There are numerous examples of net applications which includes buying carts, phrase processors, on line forms, document conversions, and scanning, on line forms, and e-mail applications like Yahoo and Gmail.

How to Work with Django

Django is used to create net programs. It is in particular meant to create a web software that connects to a database. You can also cope with consumer management, properly security, and internationalization. Some of the commonplace net packages include Disqus, Pinterest, and Instagram. You can use Django as standalone libraries although it will require extra work. That is the purpose why it isn't always really useful to use it as a standalone.

Django is a mixture of one-of-a-kind components that paintings via responding to user requests.

The first step is the request-or-reaction machine. The predominant paintings are to get hold of and return web responses. Django will accept all the requests of the URLs and return all the HTML facts to the internet browser. The page may be in simple textual content or something better. The internet requests will enter the Django software through the

URLs. The simplest entry point for any Django utility is the URLs; developers have the manipulate of the to be had

URLs. When you access the URL, Django will permit the viewing.

All your requests might be processed by using the views. Django perspectives are considered to be codes generated from Python when the URL is accessed. Views are something easy like returning a text to the consumer. The textual content may be made complex. It can be form processing, credit score card processing, and database querying. When the view has finished processing, an internet response is sent to the consumer. When net response is returned, the user can get admission to the URL at the browser they will get entry to the response. This might be an HTML net page that indicates a mixture of photos and text, and they are created using the templating system from Django. With Django facts, there's flexibility to have extra packages. You can use which you create an easy blog, cell applications, or a desktop. Django framework is powered by way of web sites like Instagram and Pinterest.

User Accounts

A user account is at the community server that is used to save the username of the computer, password, and any applicable statistics. When you have got the user account, it will permit you or no longer to connect to other computers or networks. With a network with a couple of users, you will want person accounts. A correct example of a user account is your e-mail account.

There are extraordinary styles of person money owed, irrespective of the working device that you are using. You may be capable of trace, authenticate, and monitor all the services. When you put in a running device, it creates user bills to have get admission to after the installation. After the installation, you'll have four consumer accounts; device account, outstanding consumer account, normal and visitor person account.

System account: These are accounts that might be used to get admission to resources in the system. The running system will use these accounts to know if a service is allowed to get entry to the assets or now not. When they are established, they invent relevant accounts; and after installation, the account might be capable of get admission to the needed information. If you are a network or machine administrator, you may not want to have any information approximately the debts.

Super user account: This account is privileged within the working device. When one is the use of Windows, the account is referred to as the Administrator account. When the use of Linux, the account is the basis account, and the working gadget will assist the user entire one-of-a-kind responsibilities. Tasks are like beginning services, developing and deleting new consumer accounts, putting in new software program, and changing system documents.

Regular user account: This account does not have many privileges and cannot make modifications within the device homes and files. They simplest function on obligations that they're authorized like going for walks applications, developing files, and customizing variables.

The Guest person account: This is the account that has less privilege; you will no longer be capable of change something with the gadget. The account is understood to perform temporary responsibilities like playing games, watching movies, or surfing the net. Using Windows, this account may be created after installation; and in Linux, you may need to create the account manually after installation.

The subsequent step is to recognize a way to create a person account. When you've got a couple of users the usage of the same computer, you may want to have new person money owed for every person. When using Windows, you may create several debts. Each of the person bills has its very own settings. It will assist you to manipulate the documents separately, and when every user logs in, it will likely be like their very own computer.

The first step in growing a person account is to click on START on the CONTROL PANEL then click on ADD or REMOVE person money owed. Click on CREATE A NEW ACCOUNT and select the account type. You will enter the account name after which choose the account type which you desire to create. The administrator has the privilege to create and alternate accounts and putting in applications. The distinction is a popular user can't perform such tasks. The closing step might be to click at the CREATE ACCOUNT button and close the CONTROL PANEL.

How to Style and Deploy an App

There are special deployment options that want to be taken into consideration. When an app is developed in the utility builder, it is created within the workplace. All the places of work have IDs and names; all you need is to create a software within the improvement and then installation it in production.

During deployment, you will decide wherein you want the existing ID to be inside the workplace, current HTTP server, or in growing new ones. The deployment options encompass.

You will first create a software this is expressed with the aid of quit-users.

The fine manner to installation a software is by growing an Application Express for stop users. Then sent the URL and login information to the users. It will work whilst the consumer population is tolerant and small.

You will need to apply the equal schema and workplace. You want to export after which import the utility, then set up that underneath a different application ID. This method will work whilst there are fewer adjustments to any known objects.

Use the equal schema and a different workplace, export all, after which import the applications into every other workplace. It will prevent any production and modification with the aid of developers.

Use a one of a kind schema and workspace. Export after which import the software right into a separate workplace, and install it in a separate schema.

Use an exclusive database for all variations. Export then import to another oracle utility and then deploy it to a distinctive database and schema.

To set up an app, within the configuration supervisor console, click on SOFTWARE LIBRARY. Go to APPLICATION MANAGEMENT after which select APPLICATION or APPLICATION GROUP.

Choose from a utility or software group from the install listing and click on DEPLOY.

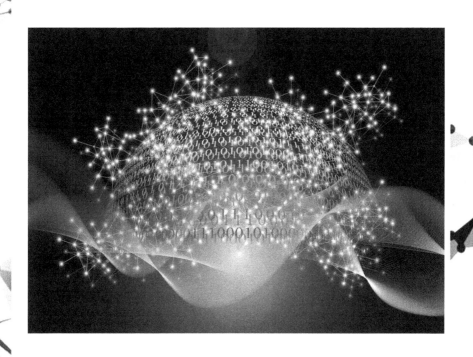

Project - 1 (Game)

Before I provide you with your first project, let me quickly shed some light on what you can expect from these projects.

Every project will be unique, as each one of us will have different ideas about how to carry out the task and execute the same. The projects will be designed to provide you with seemingly simple tasks, only to find out that you may have to do a little more than just copying and pasting blocks of code from one file to another.

Use your coding knowledge from all sources, as these will not be bound to individual chapters. Projects are where you will encounter all kinds of problems, situations, and scenarios. To solve these, or finish them successfully, you will need to use various methods right from the beginning, all the way to the end of complex matters like functions, classes, and modules.

I will be providing you with links from which you can download specific modules, libraries, or classes to help further make the process easier. You already know how to import them into your PyCharm using the "from x import y" or "import xyz" method. Try and make a simple-looking scenario complex and interesting. Continue developing these projects with advanced knowledge that you will hopefully gain after this book. A program is never truly complete. Even the best programs and software continue to be updated with newer knowledge, modules, and variations.

Keep on practicing and adding more to these projects. Who knows, you might end up with something far superior and more useful than just a message that says "Hello World" at the end.

Task:

Create a simple game of "Rock, Paper, Scissors," where the computer randomly generates value and asks the user to input their selection. The result should show whether the user wins or loses, or if it is a draw.

Requirements:

To complete this project, you will need to use the following:

Packages:

From random import randint – This will be your first line of code. Random comes pre-installed and allows you to force the computer to randomize the selection. This will help you in ensuring that every turn is unique and unpredictable.

There are quite a few ways you can complete this project. As a reference, I will share my solution for this project at the end of the book as well.

Please note that I wish to encourage you to explore the world of Python and use your genuine approaches, communicate with the community, and learn better ways to code. For this reason, I will not share the details on the

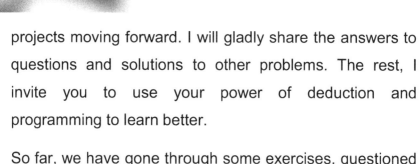

projects moving forward. I will gladly share the answers to questions and solutions to other problems. The rest, I invite you to use your power of deduction and programming to learn better.

So far, we have gone through some exercises, questioned what was right and what was not. We even initiated our very first project, which is quite challenging in all fairness. However, everything hinges on how well you understand your basics. The better you know them, the easier it will be to move from a beginner to an intermediate programmer and eventually to a skilled programmer. If you are unsure about certain aspects, it is always a good habit to revisit the concepts and revise what you have learned.

Time to say goodbye to variables and storing values and move on to our friends, the statements, and loops.

Project - 2

Time for yet another project. Since we are discussing games, create a Python program that lets the user know their astrological sign from the given date of birth. The program may seem rather easy, but once you look into the smaller details, you will soon realize that this will require you to think a little out of the box.

For this project, I will not be providing hints nor a model to follow. You already know, and you should be able to execute this one with ease and a bit of finesse as well. You do not need any special modules or packages to get this project done. All you need is a quick search on the internet to see which star sign starts when to get you going.

Through trial and error, you should be able to create a program that can work easily and exceptionally. Should you encounter issues, try and resolve them on your own instead of looking for a solution on the internet.

If such projects interest you, you can find many more by searching for "Python projects for beginners" and get started. The more projects you work on, the better you will learn. Keep an eye out for what is in demand these days and set your target to one day be able to carry out programming of a level that will get you paid handsomely.

CONCLUSION

Thank you for making it to the end of Python Crash Course. Let us hope that it was informative and able to provide you with all of the tools you need to achieve your goals whatever they may be. The objective of this is to present an introduction for the absolute beginners to machine learning and data science.

This covers the dominant machine learning paradigms, namely supervised, unsupervised, semi-supervised, and reinforcement. This explains how to develop machine learning models in general and how to develop a neural network which is a particular method of performing machine learning. It teaches how to train and evaluate their accuracy.

Python is a widely used programming language for different applications and in particular for machine learning. This covers the basic Python programming as well as a guide to use Python libraries for machine learning.

This presents machine learning applications using real datasets to help you enhance your Python programming skills as well as machine learning basics acquired through the book. These applications provide examples of developing a machine learning model for predictions using linear regression, a classifier using logistic regression and artificial neural network. Through these applications, examples of data exploration and visualization using Python are presented.

Nowadays, machine learning is used in every domain, such as marketing, health care systems, banking systems, stock market, gaming applications, among others. This book's objective is to provide a basic understanding of the significant branches of machine learning as well as the philosophy behind artificial neural networks. This also aims at providing Python programming skills for machine learning to beginners with no earlier programming skills in Python or any other programming language.

Remember that deep learning is relatively easy, contrary to collective thinking among programmers. The industry is quickly moving toward the top to take control of machines. There are lots of people who are firmly in favor of machine learning, but I have some solid reasons that deep learning is more profitable than machine learning. Practically speaking, deep learning is a subset of machine learning. It secures power and flexibility by learning the world on the basis of the database that it has stored in the backend.

It works on the back of its hidden learning architecture that consists of multiple layers with some dense layers. The data is processed through these layers where the neural networks get to work on matching the input data with the data that is stored in the databases in the backend. Upon each match, they return the output on the basis of some highly educated findings that are efficient and very well managed.

Once you have acquired the skills and understood the reasoning behind machine learning models presented in this book, you will be able to use these skills to solve complex problems using machine learning. You will also be able to easily acquire other skills and use more advanced machine learning methods. In this guide, I explained to you the basics of Python language. Learning to program is like learning another language. It takes a lot of patience, study, application, method, passion and above all perseverance.

What I can suggest is to do as much practice as possible by starting to rewrite the hundreds of examples you find in this guide. Try to memorize them and when you write the code, say it to yourself, in your mind (open bracket, close round brackets and so on). In the beginning, this helped me a lot to memorize better the various steps needed to write a program even if simple.

It is important not to feel like heroes when a program works but above all you should not be depressed when you cannot find a solution to your programming problems. The network is full of sites and blogs where you can always find a solution.

I hope that this guide has been useful for you in learning Python.

www.ingramcontent.com/pod-product-compliance
Lightning Source LLC
LaVergne TN
LVHW051244050326
832903LV00028B/2559